Chasing Rabbits & I Am...

The Art of Attainment

By *Jan Deelstra*

Chasing Rabbits & I Am

2014 © Jan Deelstra

Library of Congress Cataloging-in-Publication data:
Deelstra, Jan.
Chasing Rabbits & I Am....

First Edition
Tradepaper ISBN 13: 978-1502546449
ISBN 10: 1502546442

I. Wealth/Money Attainment II. Gestalt III. Author IV. Title

Transformational author, women's empowerment life coach, gestalt practitioner: Healing the whole of you through gestalt techniques and improved self-esteem.

Also by Deelstra:

Escaping the Chrysalis: Techniques for Self-Esteem Transformation
Blessings in the Mire: A True Story of Miracles & Recollections
Shadows Attached: Mad Woman Poetry
The Flying Game
Infinite Pie
The Mindful Path to Wellness & Beauty
Empowering Words to Enlightenment

Manufactured in the United States of America

For the *Mindful*, with gratitude.

Chapter One

Scattered Rabbits

Scattered Rabbits

The pioneer of all entrepreneurs, the late Mary Kay Ash, legendary founder of *Mary Kay Cosmetics*, offered the success tip, "If you chase too many rabbits, you'll never catch any."

The adage answers the question of why so many folks never attain desired goals, or more importantly, successfully live their true *callings*. Most of us are too busy chasing and never catching numerous metaphorical ricocheting rabbits to ever consciously place a foot on the pre-determined path of limitless potential.

How many people take the time to actually decide what one thing they want to do beyond all others, and then set about making and then following a plan of action that moves them one step each day to reach that determined destination? Have you?

It's more than a simple issue of chasing too many rabbits simultaneously, or of time management. The art of attainment is a matter of investing time and thoughtfulness to uncover personal strengths and weaknesses, to clarify values, and to hone in on desires. It may mean altering values and beliefs to correlate with those desires. It may call for a purge of self-doubt. It most definitely demands deciding on an ultimate goal, and determining which daily activities will lead to that goal. And then, what is required is the unbreakable commitment to attain the desire, expending applied daily action towards that goal.

There's no magic wand. The foundation for success must be built to support your dreams and aspirations.

Along the way, there will be barriers and collisions on the road; lessons of life. These detours are all a part of living, and are not road blocks, but are simple traffic patterns to be dealt with. Too often, we allow speed bumps to become death blows to the process of reaching the desired destination, or we are sidetracked by external stimuli and turn completely off the path never to return again to the idea of reaching any successful outcome.

Consider how many half-written novels were started years ago and were then abandoned, a discarded orphan sleeping in a desk drawer beneath piles of old bills and such. That napping brain-child may hold the key to wealth, success, and fulfillment, but it's not going to bring about nirvana as long as it's stuffed in the drawer. No publisher will ever publish what cannot be seen.

Without commitment to a clearly planned pathway to success as we have defined our success to be, we can be easily led astray to other less meaningful, less fulfilling activities. Rather than face a fast approaching deadline, we may be tempted to lounge at the pool. We may not do whatever it is that is the most effective use of our time towards the end goal. Or, we may simply overload our plates with so many activities that none lead to anything or anywhere productive. Under these conditions, like scattered rabbits, even our most cherished desires are unreachable.

Creative Avoidance is Not Creative Time...

The creative ways in which there are to avoid any task are as numerous as there are people procrastinating. Creative avoidance may be entertaining to watch, as when a deadline is approaching in a home based business and suddenly there are cookies to be baked and dogs to be washed by the CEO/Mom, but clearly this illustration indicates a lack of focus and commitment. Or take the example of that final exam that's looming in the morning, and under the guise of studying, the student is instead at the local coffee house ingesting caffeine, staying up all night, and then sleeping in far past the test date. And as a last example, envision the piles of bills scattered around the kitchen table and counters, each with a shelf-life that expired sometime last week or the week before. Rather than put butt in chair and write the checks, address the envelopes, and place the stamps on them and place them in the mail, procrastination in the form of creative avoidance demands to fill the space.

Creative avoidance is a passive-aggressive act of procrastination. It is a thin veil for hiding fear of success behind a lack of focus. Too many rabbits distract attention away from the goal line. As a habitual practice, creative avoidance is fear-based self-sabotage at its worst.

All that creativity would be better spent on creative productivity, and not just on busy-work. Being busy is not necessarily being productive. Lots of folks are as busy as pollinating bees, and yet they are going absolutely nowhere fast, even as they busily buzz from one thing to another to yet another. There may be a lot of frenzied dynamic motion taking place, but with too many undefined things taking chunks of time and energy, all that high energy is scattered towards too many activities. It dissipates into nothing. That's the syndrome of *chasing rabbits*. And if we chase too many rabbits at once, we have nothing to show for all that invested activity.

If you find yourself in the creative avoidance mode, notice
what task you are avoiding and stop. Without distractions,
be still and let your mind settle. You miss a lot unless
you're calm, so give your brain, your body, and your
emotions a rest in quiet solitude. Allow the silence to speak
to you. Take in a few deep breaths, and when you are calm,
visit the task with fully present attention. But please do not
turn this tranquility exercise into a creative means of
avoidance!

Often I hear clients, friends and family express how hard
they worked at such and such, but with little results to show
for the time and energy investment. This is usually a clear
sign of chaotic rabbit chasing syndrome.

By creating a daily list of goals to accomplish, we can take
a line-by-line approach to completing each task. Again
referring to Mary Kay Ash, take a suggestion from her
success oriented toolbox: Each night before bed, in your
day planner, write down a list of six things to accomplish
the next day. Then, the next day, methodically complete
each objective, beginning with the most difficult and
working thru the list to the easiest. Crossing through the
finished items is a great feeling of success and creates
momentum. The practice of organizing each task into a
bite-sized daily chunk helps ensure we stay on track
towards our chosen destination. Without this organized
plan of prioritizing the steps necessary to reach our goal,
there is slim chance we'll accomplish anything of real
substantial value. With this practice, we are encouraged by
every completed step we cross through.

As a caveat, do schedule in fun and recreation. Nobody likes a dullard, and recreational time feeds creativity. Play and laughter are the balance for responsibility and bring about fulfilled living.

Play has received an unearned reputation as being a time waster on the opposite side of the success net. Investing time in play is a crucial factor in staving off burnout. Play also provides increased happy hormones that keep our minds sharp and our wit-muscles in shape. I like to think of play as a workout for the mind; no less important than a trip to the gym. And when it's time to chase the chosen rabbit, we want shapely wits.

Similarly, it's imperative to schedule time with those who stimulate your intellect and challenge your mindset; in short, spend time with those who cause you to think. The mind is a muscle that thrives on being called into use so make use of it often. Particularly, the brain develops when it must fully devote to sifting through criteria and solving the sundry challenges of one specific charge. Adding in associations with other masterminds provides a synergistic effect that leads to greater thoughts that lead to great inventions, creations, concepts, and outcomes. Whether practiced alone or with others who cause your brain to engage, utilize the magnificence of the mind.
Brainstorming is an art form to perfect, because when the rainbow comes out after the brainstorm, the strength of clarity glimmers in the aftermath.

My professional calling includes being a long-term Gestalt practitioner, being a certified practitioner of Neuro Linguistic Programming (NLP), being certified in Hypnotherapy, being practiced in Emotional Freedom Technique (EFT), and being certified as a life coach, among other degrees and certifications. These degrees and certifications were achieved individually, one-by-one, with a clearly defined plan and daily action steps. Particularly because there are similarities between NLP and hypnosis certification, to attempt to become certified in both at the same time would been disastrous. I would not have become proficient or certified in either skill. It would have been a mess, a convoluted mix which, in the end, had no merit or substance. Without a plan to achieve each individual skill, and without daily action, the challenge of reaching the finish line would have been like chasing scattering rabbits with no successful outcome.

Not strictly as a result of this diverse training and of hanging my life coaching shingle, clients often come to me wanting to make changes in many areas of their life. This is fine; in fact, it's great. But to ensure lasting and profound transformation mandates a precise clarity. And clarity demands that each goal or desire be focused on individually. One issue or challenge at a time must be addressed. Attempting to create change in several areas at once dilutes the process and, like trying to chase too many rabbits at once, in the end, little or nothing is effectively accomplished.

As an example of this, when I create a hypnotic recording for a client, that client is instructed to calm the chaos in the mind, and to listen to the recording every night before bed, for at least 21 days. It takes most of us about three weeks to change or develop a habit, so the 21 nights of replaying the hypnosis recording is generally most effective. It would not be effective, if on nights one and five, the client listened to a pre-recorded session about *being a money magnet*, and on nights two and seven, listened to recorded messages about *confidence* or *weight loss*. Listening for three weeks to a recording about attaining an optimal state of wellness, and then for the next three weeks moving onto another individual challenge such as confidence building, or financial wellbeing would reap best results.

As a short side note, I do not encourage weight "loss," as we humans are programmed to *find* whatever we have *lost*. When we've misplaced our keys, for example, we may wake in the middle of the night suddenly remembering that suit coat pocket. Our subconscious mind has retraced the path to find the keys even as we sleep. For circumventing this innate ability to find what is lost, I prefer using the term "achieving an optimal goal weight," as that goal weight is something that we can strive *for* rather than *against*. We tend to respond best when we are actioning *for* something, than when we are *against* it. Given that partiality for attaining as opposed to moving away from a goal, it's most effective to create a plan *for* reaching an optimal condition. This is perhaps never more essential than in the pursuit of the optimal physique, and just as importantly, in the quest of seeing that elusive magic number on the bathroom scale.

A cutout picture of the body you seek, with your head pinned onto it and then taped to the refrigerator door is much more of an incentive than is counting calories and denying yourself a carb once in a while. The visual image of the ideal you is planted in your brain each time you look in that direction. That daily dose of consciousness helps bring about the change you seek. And in case you're of the opposite end of the body image spectrum, this technique works well for body building too.

Chasing Rabbits & I Am...

By Jan Deelstra

Personally, I know three people who, thru single-mindedly focusing on one rabbit, each manifested their individual ideals of the perfect body. Simply through repetitious visualization of the magazine cutouts they'd taped to the fridge, coupled with awareness of what they ate and how much physical movement they enjoyed, they each attained health and their idea of perfection. Of course, having the images front and center each time the urge to munch hits is probably a strong characteristic of the process for success! Guilt can be a great motivator for helping keep us on the track to the destination!

For this reason, whether regarding health, or in pursuit of any goal, consider getting an accountability partner and encouraging each other to stay on track. Keep in mind the higher success rate of focusing on one specified goal at a time, and transform one challenging area at a time. Being partners in similar quests adds a synergistic element that increases momentum and brings about an element of competitive fun to the achievement process. Play nice, be supportive and celebrate each other's successes as they come. The buddy system is a winner's system. And it costs nothing to join forces with a kindred spirit seeking the same or similar life transformations.

The results you are seeking come fastest and stay longer when each challenge receives ample time in the spotlight. Be patient as you thoroughly excavate for ills and benefits. When allowed a significant timeframe for achieving a clearly planned, mapped, and results-driven outcome, success is ensured. Transformation may take days, weeks, or even months, but in the end, the outcome is achieved and embedded in the subconscious mind, and so it sticks. It is the new normal.

Let's take the hypothetical stance that you have entered into sessions with me because you are feeling a sense of separation from others. You experience life as a spectator sport, living from the sidelines. On the surface, colleagues and friends see you as a successful business woman, but inside, you are experiencing feelings of insecurity, or you're asking, "Is this all there is?" Regardless of your accomplishments, you're not feeling all that *successful* despite your outward appearance. Beginning with a private conversation to gather information and clarify your desired outcome, we would create a plan unique to your specific needs. We may incorporate some NLP in the process, or maybe we would decide jointly to add some hypnotic sessions into that plan. If so, we would create a recording of the hypnosis, and you would be instructed to listen to the recording of your hypnosis session each night for 21 nights.

After these 3 weeks, if you had reached the degree of satisfaction you were seeking, we would either conclude the coaching services, or you may opt to move onto another challenge such as relationships, or finances, etc. It's all very subjective and specialized to provide the most enhanced empowerment in the shortest time. However, if we tried to transform relationships, finances, build confidence, and also deal with feelings of a sense of separation in one fell swoop, like an owl with greased talons, we would likely miss the rabbit. Some key transformational milestones would go untouched. In the flurry, you may receive a great deal of revolutionary success, but you would receive even greater successes over a structured, more focused step-by-step program.

Given that there are 52 weeks in a year, and it takes 3 weeks to implement each change, imagine the level of full transformation that could be achieved in one year. The possibilities are near endless!

Now, on the other side of the possibility coin, imagine a full year passes without any consciously intended changes to your daily, monthly, yearly routine.... You continue living your life pretty much as you have been for as long as you can remember. Which image of *you* is most enticing?

Here's yet another side to that theme: Several of my VIP clients who are addressing challenges which have roots in poor self-esteem have undergone extreme transformation in only one day, and in more than one area of challenges. This is because we have spoken about the underlying challenges and symptoms, and have defined the desired outcome. Then, we get to the deepest roots and pull the weeds of doubt. We then immediately plant the new seeds of confidence and cultivate success with a clearly detailed action plan. There may be weeds to pull, and seeds to plant, and a lot of rabbits to chase, but by going after one success at a time, we manage to take control and achieve multiple planned outcomes as rapidly as those rabbits can run!

Similarly, participants in the intensive group coaching events experience rapid, profound, and lasting transformations. This is partially due to the undeniable synergistic effect that takes place in the group settings. The transformational vibration is a palpable energy in these group situations. But not everyone is emotionally equipped to participate in the intensity of such high speed, high energy group programs. Although the results are unforgettable, and frequently result in life-long friendships forged in the shared setting, not everyone is suitable for that deeply personal level of commitment to such a fast-paced premium transformational experience. There are tears, laughter, and a lot of emotion being released. In that release comes the freedom and energy burst that occurs with liberation from the past pains. Not everyone is comfortable sharing such a personal journey with others. And that's okay. In fact, before you reach the end of this book, you'll hear me say often, *it's perfect.*

Chapter Two

The "I Am" of You

Chapter Two

I Am That I Am...

The colorful axiom of chasing too many rabbits and not catching anything gets me to thinking that every single time we utter a sentence beginning with, "I am....," we are sending a message of our identity to the universe to be answered in return. Please hear and carefully use your words! Stop saying things like, "I am sick and tired," or "I am so sick of..." or, "I can't stand...," or even, "You're killing me!" These carelessly used words are affirming and manifesting dis-ease (or death).

Own your life's results by intentionally speaking only the words which will support and not sabotage your desired outcome! With the rabbit syndrome in mind, send out a clearly detailed message of your #1 intention. Begin the affirmed intention with, "I am," and fill in the blank with your intended result. Use this process each morning and throughout the day as you intend yourself right into the life of your dreams.

Here's something to consider: Whenever you utter the two words "I am," you are calling the name of God. Stay with me here; don't run off just yet. God said, "I am that I am." And each time you use those words, "I am," you too are defining the god-ness of yourself. As example: I am, fat, thin, sick, well, weak, strong, rich, poor, etc. all carry a unique vibration which is being called out with a distinct energetic charge. It is not possible to be rich, for instance, if one is referring to the self and seeing oneself as, "I am poor." It's as if the "god" in you is being called out as the god of "scarcity." No amount of meditating, or earnest intention, or manifesting techniques, or uttering affirmations, and not even any amount of prayer will change this.

The action that will change the condition of impoverishment and lack is changing your personal vibration to align with the higher frequency of the abundant state which you desire to be. In fact, unless you raise your vibration to that of the desired vibratory state of your ideal, nothing improves. Your attempts at mastering the law of attraction to manifest abundance fall flat.

Consider that your divinity is in your transmission. Your soul resonance is the frequency you emit, and the effects of your energetic broadcast are an exact match. Clearly hear and feel the "I am" in your dialog and call in your highest potential with intention to be that higher self. Manifest your ideal life, and your ideal self through the transmission of the energetic magnets, *I am abundance. I am healthy. I am whole and complete. I am worthy. I am a goddess.*

Humans Being

If the, "I am" concept doesn't quite agree with you, it may be easier to swallow from this perspective: We are all humans *being* something or being multiple things. We are humans being poor, being wealthy, being victims, being heroes, being sick, being well, being fat, being fit, being lazy, being dynamic, being failures, being successes, being jocks, being couch potatoes, being kind, being curious, etc.

We wear many hats throughout the day, as we are *being* our different roles (mom, wife, friend, employee, cook, chauffeur, etc.). As we are being these roles, we are calling into being the effects of the frequency which we are broadcasting through the frequency of how we are being. If we are humans being mindful, being well, being wealthy, being consciously creative, etc., we are then living in the energy of that particular being state. Likewise, if we are being victims, or being martyrs, being judgmental, being angry, being impoverished, being depressed, etc., we are broadcasting fear-based frequencies into the ethers.

We are then being far from the possibility of our divinity. We are not being our enlightened self. In any case, what we are being is being supported by the universe as it seeks to mirror our primary resonance. We get what we give.

To manifest anything, we must be aligned energetically with the vibrational frequency of that which we are seeking, and most importantly, we must believe and trust that whatever we are seeking is also seeking us. What we seek to manifest must be in alignment with our spiritual, emotional, physical, and thoughts. It is essential to condition our self to allow the flow inward. And it is imperative that we are ready and open to receive, and that we are an energetic match for delivery.

As we step into our authentic alignment –into the *I Am* of our choice, as we calm the rabbits and hold that desired resonating vibration by *being* the desired condition for increasingly longer durations, we create the 'beingness' of that which we are calling. We are literally manifesting our divinity by consciously stepping into the *feeling* of being our ideal self.

Holding that *I Am beingness* vibration for as little as thirty seconds throughout the day brings to fruition great change. The small act of resonating for several seconds raises our vibration and also raises the allowance factor incrementally. Our inner worthiness thermostat in our subconscious mind is raised to accept the state we are manifesting. The emotion attached to the image of the ideal self or ideal life is the frequency emitted. The more intense the emotion mustered, the more intense the frequency radiated, and the more accurate the result.

Like Magic Only Better

Try an experiment this week. Take thirty seconds out of each morning as soon as you awaken. Do this before you get out of bed, and when you are still relaxed. Decide on one particular 'rabbit' you would like to snare. Let's use the example that you are intent on manifesting one-thousand-dollars. Of course, you can decide for yourself what to manifest; this is only for the sake of example. With your goal in mind, for thirty-seconds in the morning, close your eyes and feel your whole self as you experience yourself as the receiver of one-thousand-dollars.

Breathe in the feeling of joy that you experience as you successfully manifest this amount. Feel the joyful knowing in your soul that you can manifest whatever you set your sights on. Smile with your eyes closed, and sense how your face feels as the mouth turns up. Notice that warmth of happiness that washes through your body as you experience the manifestation of your conscious desires. Hold the feelings for thirty full seconds, or more. Savor them.

Without attachment, notice and feel that vibration in your body, in your mind, and in your spirit for thirty-seconds or longer if you're enjoying the process. Notice the difficulty or the ease of holding the emotion for the suggested time frame. Is it tough to stay in the moment? Does your mind wander off like irreverent rabbits? Without judging, notice your body, your thoughts, your feelings as you broadcast and receive on this frequency.

If you find it difficult to mindfully be in the thirty-second process, take a short break and calm the mind. When you are ready, try it again. Eventually you will be capable of moving effortlessly and easily into this practice as a form of self-hypnosis. You can even run through this as you wait in grocery store lines or pump gas.

Repeat the technique throughout the day whenever you think about it, and then again just prior to bedtime. It's like magic, only better because it really works at a molecular level to clarify and speed up the fruitions.

Manifesting Love and Fear

A key factor in perfecting the art of manifestation begins with consciousness of your inner dialog, as words have creative power, but with an additional awareness of the emotion attached. There is no way to *not* manifest. Irrespective of if we are aware or are not aware of the role our words and emotions play in manifestation, and regardless of whether or not what's being called in is what we would consciously choose to manifest, we are each manifesting all day long and probably even as we sleep. We manifest from an intensity of emotion whether that emotion is fear-based or love-based. Cognizance is Queen! Developing an automatic awareness of each emotion we feel and every word we think and utter is an empowering tool for conscious creation. When the act of self-awareness becomes ingrained, you may find yourself observing high stakes manifestations in response to the love-based transmissions you're broadcasting.

Consider something or someone you really loath, anyone or anything that leaves a really bad taste in your mouth when you think about the experience of it/them. Personally, I love broccoli, but if that works for you, draw on that loathing emotion for this example. Maybe it is someone who you feel 'wronged' you in the past. Feel the emotion attached to your choice of experiences. Notice how the emotion of loathing expresses itself in your body. Take note of your heart rate, or your facial expression, of your fists, of your posture, of any physical aches or pain throughout your body, of your body temperature as you draw on the emotion of loathing. In your mind's eye, see the energy of loathing being broadcast into the ethers. It radiates away from your heart and ripples far and long into the future where it meets with the mirror that reflects it all back to you.

Chasing Rabbits & I Am...
By Jan Deelstra

Take a ten minute break and drink some water. Allow your mind to be calm and still. Breathe in deeply, and consciously exhale, releasing the stress you've just created through your thoughts and your emotions. Before progressing any further, get centered and relaxed. Clear the remnants of the negativity to make room for the next step in this exercise.

Now that you are ready, envision someone you cherish, and love unconditionally. If you've not experienced that depth of love, imagine it. Pull queues from smarmy movies or love songs, or think about puppies or bunnies or new born babies if it helps create the mental scene and evoke the emotion we're going for here. Take a few minutes and really allow that love to swell in your heart. Feel the emotional charge surge throughout your entire body flushing you with love. Watch it radiate outward far into the ethers. Notice the smile that has crept over your face as you recall this profound love. Maybe there is even a little touch involved and your heart races with anticipation. Feel the tingle. Experience the excitement of that love-based emotion as it swells in you and then radiates further still rippling outward into the limitless ethers. Now picture that intense emotion of love as it meets its match and mirrors the intense love-based energetic current, returning it to you in a perfect circuit of energy.

In both these imaginary scenarios, that's the power you have to manifest. It's that simple. And it's not imaginary. It's the *law of attraction*, and loved-based or fear-based, like it or not, you're living it every second of every day. You are the co-creator of your life experience. Isn't that just about the most empowering thing you could ever consider *being*? Doesn't that knowledge awaken you with a whole new awareness of the "I Am" of you?

Environmental Energy Emissions

We've all known someone who whines constantly, someone who complains about everything, or someone who constantly lives in drama. As if crafted by Hollywood writers, dramatic events always seem to happen to these folks. Just like actors, these folks are pretending. They are pretending to have no say in the matter of their life events; they are chronically *being* victims.

The victim role is the identity they are cultivating, whether consciously or not. Please do not feel sorry for them. Your pity and attention to their drama is only fertilizer for continued dysfunction. Stop watching. Stop listening.

But this is a _____ (family member, childhood friend, etc.) you protest. For whatever reason, we generally offer more leniencies to the dysfunctions of friends and family. It's as if there is a separate blueprint of acceptable behaviors for those closest to us. We may harshly judge strangers, and even co-workers, but friends and family receive special consideration for their lack of evolution. We may even "feel sorry for them."

Here's the real deal: All that negative energy is spewed into the ethers attracting more negative energy in return. When you're involved you are in the direct firing line of the negative force. It's tough to protect yourself from that sort of attack, and before long, you too will be radiating and circulating the toxins. Have you spent time with a real "downer" and then noticed how hard it was to not buy into the negativity? Or perhaps you have a close friend or relative who seems to look constantly for reasons to be offended. Within minutes of being in this person's environment you catch yourself churning out poison too. It's contagious!

Cease to further cultivate the dysfunction under the guise of support. Withdraw your time and energy and misguided caring. By ceasing to foster the negativity, you are actually empowering them, so please, change the channel. By placing your time and attention on the, "woe is me" stories, you are offering incentive to grow more *woe*. A more empowering response for all parties is for you to focus on the positives of that which you are now consciously creating for yourself. Share your progress as an inspiring role model. Own your role in your own story of success and liberation, and be sure to include some comedy and adventure and a little less drama. Consciously construct you fabulous life story. And who knows, maybe they too will start to write their own big hit.

Being Bearably Light

The best formula for enhancing the lives of the masses is to <u>be</u> the light, not the darkness. You cannot get sick enough or poor enough to help anyone, but you can be well and live an abundant life and show others how to do the same. Your life can be the poster-child, the demonstration of consciously crafted success.

Consider this: You have a mental image of who you are, and you project this image as your identity. It is the way others perceive who you are *being*. Now suddenly, you change your image, your behavior, maybe even your values; others notice. Those who notice may want to keep you the way they have always known you. Humans like things consistent. Overall, we don't like things to change; change upsets the ostensible balance, even when things are actually out of balance.

Many acquaintances may not be supportive when you change because it causes a shift in power, and a shift in their energetic footing; your shift means they don't know where they stand. Others may attempt to keep you from changing, using manipulation, guilt, or even physical restraint. This happens when one partner outgrows a relationship and attempts to leave, but is hindered. Be prepared for this: When you change, there *will* be resistance somewhere from someone. Let it be. Give it no energy. Stay the course. Eventually the naysayers will grow weary and stop trying to recreate the past. Some will change with you. Some will not, and those will be left behind. That's okay. In fact, that's perfect.

The Universe also takes note when you change. We want the Universe to notice the change, and to support our new vision. And it will rise up to meet the new improved version, as long as the change is not too drastic. True even if it's an improvement, your subconscious mind, and the responsive Universe must get on board with this new image you are trying on. It must be believable and in line with your values and beliefs as your subconscious knows those traits to be. If the new image is authentic, the subconscious mind and the Universe have no trouble accepting the identity because it aligns with your core. If not, you'll be back to your old ways almost immediately.

Don't try to trick your subconscious mind; It will get even.

If the new image is not in alignment with your core values, your self- image, and with your authentic calling, the image is not going to be believable. When the new image is unbelievable, no amount of forcing is going to get that new you to be accepted by your subconscious mind, or by the Universe. And when your gate-keeper, your subconscious mind, is not on board, you can bet there will be resistance to change, in the form of self-sabotage. As for the Universe, it will fully respond to exactly what your subconscious mind accepts. When your self-conscious mind is aligned with your desires, the Universe fully cooperates to bring you the resonance of your transmission. Ease into your new image using the thirty second practice and the 21 day rule of systematically implementing change, one rabbit at a time.

Answer for yourself:

Does your mind accept your image?
Is your spirit on board?
Is your energetic vibration in alignment with your values?
Is your energetic vibration in alignment with the image being projected?
Is this a "make-believe" you, or is this the authentic core persona of who you are at a spiritual level?
Can you calm the chaos and still your mind to allow for the peaceful state necessary for manifestation to occur?

We know now that even as little as thirty seconds at a time of consciously holding a high vibration is enough to form the habit which eventually permanently increases the speed of our vibrations. Gone is the excuse of not having time to create the life you've so long desired. We can all find thirty seconds, multiple times per day, to imprint our new life.

What may be more difficult is quieting the mind chatter and allowing our mind to be like still waters, tranquil and receptive to change. This is a practice to perfect. A calm mind is a creative mind that supports health and well-being. All those running rabbits must be nestled into their holes, for chaos to quell and mindfulness to resume. The thirty seconds allows for the dust to settle over the rabbit holes and the energy to shift to a more effective point. You reap much from stillness. And when you are manifesting your ideal image, the mind must be onboard. Not only are you creating your ideal self-image and desired life experience, you are also acknowledging your calling.

When we are fully aligned –mind, body, spirit, and core values, we are living our *calling*. And ONLY when we are aligned are we capable of actually mastering the art of manifesting. Until the point of mastery we may realize small successes, but unless there is full acceptance from self, the wins will be short lived. This truth is clearly illustrated in the example of 'nouveau riche' coming into money, and almost immediately ending up worse off for the experience. Unless and until there is alignment, and without a matching vibrational charge, there can be no lasting sustainment of the success.

I AM wealthy, is an effective meditation and/or affirmation only when aligned with our inner values, with our sense of personal value, and when we are truly experiencing a sense of wealth. In contrast, if we are actually experiencing lack, we must place our frequency on the higher vibration of gratitude and abundance. Consciously, we must experience our vibration of the higher love-based frequency which is a feeling of being at peace, and trusting the perfection of the universe and the law of attraction. With incongruence there will be no wealth match.

Your *beingness* must be consistently and authentically defined as the state of *I am* (that which you desire to create). I use wealth creation and self-actualization as examples most often as these seem to be universal themes. But creation is creation; regardless of what is being created the steps are the same. Staying positive and stating affirmations is not the answer to manifesting if it's an artificial act, or if you're actually emitting miserable emotions, or if you are unbelieving. Your conscious mind will fight against anything it knows to be untrue. Staying authentic, broadcasting while in a heightened energetic state of genuine gratefulness regardless of circumstances, and believing in your power to manifest whatever you seek are the principle keys to a good life. We all have "bad" moments in life that help us appreciate the good times through contrast. Those learning episodes need not be translated into *bad lives*.

Rabbits and Tigers and Bears, Oh NO!

The following questions are presented as an in-depth assignment to be completed over the course of one week. As a step towards enlightenment, invest the time to journal one or more of these self-awareness questions daily until you've answered each with attention to how you *feel* physically, mentally, and emotionally as you respond:

Overall:

> *Describe your ideal self in detail.*
> *Choose 5 words to fill in the blank: I Am_____.*
> *What emotions are you typically broadcasting?*
> *What are you most fearful of?*
> *What are your top five dislikes?*
> *What are your top five likes?*
> *What one thing turns you one most? Why?*
> *What's your least favorite emotion? Why?*
> *How does your voice sound?*
> *How do you most often dress?*
> *What is your educational level?*
> *What's your favorite word?*
> *What's your least favorite word?*
> *How do you live?*
> *Is your home reflective of your self-image?*
> *What are your three greatest talents?*
> *Are your values in line with your defined new role?*
> *What is your bank account balance?*
> *Describe your five closest friends.*
> *How do you feel in this new image you're creating?*
> *When you look in the mirror, are you congruent?*
> *Complete this sentence: I am most comfortable_____.*
> *Complete this sentence: I am least comfortable_____.*
> *Chasing rabbits describes me_____.*

Visit http://www.JanDeelstra.com to download support wares for your life journey.

Chapter Three

Mindfulness MATTER$

Mindfulness MATTER$

"The greatest reward in becoming a millionaire is not the amount of money that you earn. It is the kind of person that you have to become to become a millionaire in the first place." -Jim Rohn

There is much wisdom, and there is such a profound clue to wealth achievement in the above quote by the late millionaire- maker, Jim Rohn. We have all heard stories about those folks who come into large sums of money before they are ready to receive it: Lottery winners and beneficiaries frequently end up in worse circumstances after the gain than they ever were before.

We probably all believe that we would be different. If we were to win the lottery, we wouldn't fritter the booty away….

But what is the determining factor in whether one wins and continues to live the good life, or if one wins and the "good life" is short lived, repelled by a lack of readiness?

The answer is, "mindset." Until and unless the mindset is one of unwavering deserving, any windfalls will run quickly through life like water through a sieve. The personal wealth thermostat must be congruent with any wealth that flows in or that flow will soon become a dried up stream bed.

Chasing Rabbits & I Am...
By Jan Deelstra

1. *Are you worthy of living a life of abundance?*
2. *What lessons did your parents pass on to you?*
3. *What self-image do you hold and project?*
4. *Is your self-image congruent with the ideal you?*
5. *Are your words in line with your personal value?*
6. *Do you currently respect the money that comes to you?*
7. *Do you spend wisely, consistently?*
8. *Is there ever or never "enough"?*
9. *Does your spirituality affect your right to attract money?*
10. *Does God want you to be rich?*

Let's take each question in order:

1. *Are you worthy of living a life of abundance?*

This question is where the roots of all scarcity and/or abundance begin to grow. Without an inner feeling of both self-worth and of being worthy to receive, money, love, and joy are not going to be attracted. If by chance some event results in an inflow of riches in these areas, the abundant conditions will quickly be cut off by an inner block. What have you embraced about your self-worth? Candidly answer this question of abundance worthiness in the privacy of your own thoughts. If you do not feel worthy of love, wealth, or happiness, look inside to the place where you learned that stifling lesson of non-support. Really look over the lesson: What do you get from holding onto an undesirable concept that doesn't support your highest desires? Consciously re-write the message of worth to support you now.

2. What lessons did your parents pass on to you?

Caregivers generally do their best, and are not usually malicious in passing on dysfunction. However, children are malleable, and are susceptible to everything around them. My own childhood was fraught with overt opinions and sentiments of *never enough*, or of contrasts between *them* (the "fortunate wealthy who lived in the all brick homes on the east side") and *us* (the unfortunate who lived in city dwellings or lived on the west side). Economic lines of demarcation between *them* and *us* were apparently set, if not in stone, then in bricks and zip codes. The message was one of shame at not being as good as, as worthy as, based solely on money and the chance of birth. But somehow, that childhood lesson of errors morphed into a monster that branded me as not worthy. There was never enough money, or love, or humor, or security, or wholeness to life. Scarcity was the life pool I was born into, and in my child's perception, I was an embarrassment. When I finally recognized my internalized scarcity beliefs and lack of self-worth, I became mindful of my inner dialog and ardent in my actions to be more than I had ever believed possible. Without delay, I clarified my values and my beliefs. I converted to diligently creating my own new empowering head-speak, meditating daily on a new mindset of *gratitude* and *plenty*. You too may want to identify your messages, and then mindfully decide what your mindset will be.

3. What self-image do you hold and project?

Do you look like a millionaire? Do you appear to be a success? Does your posture, smile, health, clothing, home, automobile, and self-image accurately portray the 'abundant successful you' or does it more closely bring to mind the wrinkled and shoddy image of a college dropout who has given up on life? As you project, the universal vibration attracts back a direct match, so beware of what you are attracting through your appearance and the condition of your belongings. If your car hasn't been washed since 1963, and your shirt is fraying around the button holes, grab a bucket and some water and use that shirt as a rag to wash your car. If you haven't cleaned your closets for over a year, get in there and thin the herd of worn-out, outdated belongings. Clear the way for the new improved vibe to flow in. It doesn't cost anything to be clean and organized. And when you look around at a clean and organized environment, when you step into a clean car, when you invest a bit of tender loving care on yourself and your surroundings, you will have a lilt in your step and will attract accordingly. Hold yourself to that higher standard and you will become that higher standard.

4. Is your self-image congruent with the ideal you?

This question reinforces the previous question about self-image, but is about how you *feel*, rather than about how others see you. If your feelings are congruent with your desired 'perfect you' then you are on the right track to claiming your divinely chosen life experience. Feeling abundant joy in all areas of life, looking in the mirror and seeing a higher state of being in your reflection, feeling deserving, and feeling secure in your self reinforces that ideal image and attracts the matching essence. We all recognize the psychological difference in when we are feeling our best and are at the top of our game, versus when we are not feeling our best. Being aligned mind, body, and spirit means to be congruent in thoughts, emotions, physicality, and at a spiritual core. Without the feeling of congruent alignment of the whole self, there will not be a successful transformation. How could there be? The laws of attraction states that what is to be manifested must be believable. We see it manifest only when we believe it.

5. *Are your words in line with your personal value?*

Words have creative power. Words start and end wars, tenderly encourage and support or brutally desecrate. Words wound or heal, express a full spectrum of emotions, create movements, educate, intimidate, create sides, and determine outcomes. Your words to yourself are the driving force in your ultimate success or failure. Over decades of counseling and coaching, I've heard more negative self-deprecation coming from clients than I've heard supportive inner dialog. Women especially, seem to avoid any words that might be misconstrued as egotistical. As a result, many women shun compliments, verbally abuse themselves, and make ill-advised negative comments about their own appearance, skills, and value. It's time for this self-deprecation to cease. It's time to turn negative self-statements into positive affirmative thoughts and speak that builds self-esteem and is supportive. It's time to value the self as if she were a fragile newborn, eager to learn from the master (you). Vow to first, hear your words, and second, vow to express only self-supporting prose to you. And while we're visiting this subject, here's a little fodder for thought: Everything you see in others and say about them is a magnet which brings it all back to you, so seek to see the positive traits and speak only of the best of all. If you see it in others, it's a part of you, whether you like it or not. And most of every communication is based on projections* of what the participants of the conversations are feeling about themselves.

*To learn more about projections, go to the end of this book for information on where to purchase the award winning inspirational book, *Escaping the Chrysalis.*

6. *Do you currently repel or attract the flow?*

Money is energy, just as is everything. How you respond to that energy determines whether that energy is repelled or attracted. The same is true of relationships. What are you attracting and what are you repelling? Compare your relationships against your relationship with money. Do you see any glaring correlations? Is your cash stuffed into pockets and wallets in haphazard fashion? Are your relationships a mess? Do you give control of your money to bankers and not address it again until you receive an over-draft notice because you weren't paying attention? If so, money will stop coming to you.

Do you give control of your affairs over to your partner? The same behavior of handing over control of your affairs and not addressing them again until a crisis condition surfaces leaving you to wonder what went wrong appears in relationships because *how we do anything is how we do everything.*

On the other hand, if you hoard the money when it's a currency meant to circulate, you also are blocking the energetic flow. Similarly, trying to 'hoard' your relationship, keeping your love held captive, or being hidden away in your relationship like a collected trophy will choke the life out of it and of you. Love will stop coming to you just as sure as money ceases to come in when it's not respected.

Balance means not only balancing your checkbook; it also means taking note of the natural ebb and flow rhythm of energy throughout all areas of your life, and acting accordingly. When in a draught, conserve and look for fresh ideas to allow more in. Find inspiration in unusual places. And when it is high tide and abundance in love, joy and money abounds, it doesn't mean it's time to squander, but rather that it's time to adjust and take care of things. Respect the nature of energy for the valuable tool it is.

Know where your energy flow is and keep an eye on *balance*. Regarding money energy, treat it with respect, not like it is a hot iron that will burn through your pocket if you don't spend it hastily. Your money is for investing in you, and is for improving your life, and for bettering the lives of others through your consciously chosen contributions to causes you care about. It is not meant for chasing shiny rabbits, nor is it a tool for making you feel lesser than or greater than the Jones family. Like it or not, money is an energy that can do much good in the right hands, or lead to much pain in the wrong hands. Your job is to decide which hand you're playing.

Regarding relationships, whether you are at ebb or at flow, respect and appreciate your relationships. They are organic living things that require attention to keep them alive. And if you discover that a relationship has truly died, don't stick around with all that dead energy. Clear the air, and make way for something new and rewarding.

7. *Do you spend wisely, consistently?*

Most of us didn't grow up with "wise spending" at the core of our teachings because most of us didn't grow up with parents with that level of financial awareness. For boomers in particular, our parent's expectation was a retirement account that paid a stipend after about twenty-five years or service to a blue collar job. Wise spending just meant we weren't buying minks instead of milk. It meant we were not at the race track betting on Brown Betty when the kids needed shoes. The stock market was something for others who wore black, navy, and pinstriped suits.

Truly, the only market I knew about was the one at the corner that sold penny candy. Wise spending was the admonishment from my mother to not blow the whole dollar allowance on a bag of marshmallows and a quart of cola…but we did. And we indulged in both treats at the same time because it was so fun to feel the frothing white explosion from our mouths when the two sweets were mixed and came gurgling out. To the observer, holding a mouthful of marshmallow and then gulping coke and watching the explosion may have not been wise spending. But it was a cheap price to pay for the hours of fun and giggles we had.

But *wise spending*? That was something government officials fought over, and still do with apparently little to no agreement or success. So ask yourself this: Are you a wiser spender than is your country's leadership or do the rabbits run wild? What is the culture of spending in the local area in which you live? Are you placing bets at the track when you might do more good to be writing that novel you've long dreamt of writing?

Perhaps we would do better to use the term conscious spending as opposed to wise spending. A little mindfulness of where our dollars are flowing, a larger awareness of the politics of those who own the corporations we are supporting when we spend our dollars at a particular store, is empowering. Regardless of your government's debt, you vote with your spending. Each cent you spend at any venue is supporting corporations and shareholders who own the venue. Wise spending then is awareness of how you contribute to society with your choices of where and how you spend. Be not only a wise spender, be an educated one.

8. *Is there ever or never "enough"?*

I have a friend who makes a good living from a business she started long ago, and which operates at a level of near zero debt. She quickly took her company past the six-figure mark. Still, she frequently complains that, "there is never enough." Honestly, I admit to having wished she would go to a third-world country and experience first-hand the lack in other parts of the world. Then, I surmise, maybe she would acknowledge there is more than enough abundance in her life! It's this habit of lack that drives her pursuit of success, but it's the same habit that keeps her stuck in the mindset of lack. There will never be enough until she begins to express gratitude for all that she has. Her mindset stops her from taking calculated risks, even though she is a conservative otherwise intelligent woman. That prudence borders on a poverty mindset and keeps her from making worthwhile philanthropical donations, and holds her back from investing in educational courses that would catapult her to the next level of her success. She does see that her wealth thermostat is stuck at a level which mimics that of her mother. Although that's not a terribly bad place to be financially, the fear-based stress my friend puts onto herself to aspire to more while seeing only lack, may lead her to an early grave.

What we focus on expands, so affirming there is always enough, and supporting worthy causes raises the bar of consciousness and attracts more for which to be grateful. It's an important awareness that may be life-saving.

9. *Does your spirituality affect your right to attract money?*

I'd retire early in Paris if I had a dollar for each time I heard a client cite Mother Theresa as the role model for poverty. Here's the truth: Mother Theresa attracted multiple millions of dollars in contributions which she used to help others in need.

Now here's another truth about wealth: You can never get poor enough to help someone else, but your monetary contribution can do much good.

You were not born to be a martyr. You're not a saint. I say this with respect and with love in my soul for you and for your divine potential. You deserve to be rich, and starting now, wherever you are, make a contribution to a cause that lights you up. And don't stop with the idea of contributing cash; give also of your time, energy and talents.

There are myriad ways to effect positive change. And there are always going to be those less fortunate. Regardless of financial status, we can all make a positive difference.

Here's another truth: There may be no better way to get the flow moving, than to give. So take a time out and determine where you wish to invest your time, your money, and your energy. Start the flow at the level which you are compelled to begin, but start today.

10. *Does God want you to be rich?*

Answer this question with that inner truth/lie detector in your gut and with self-love in your heart. With your sanest emotions at front and center, contemplate God. For just a second, set aside any dogma which may taint your authentic response. God wants you to be rich. Clearly this is the truth. Otherwise, why would we live in such an abundant universe where we are truly blessed to be residing? To turn our back on the opportunity of that abundant blessing would be to deny that we are each a cog in something greater than our individual self. When one of us prospers, we all benefit, as long as we are cognizant of our connections, and pay it forward. It's a cycle of creation which perpetuates our species and our universe.

Without exception, God –however you define the Source of all Creation, wants you to be rich. As we grow into abundance, we are transforming into a higher version of our self. We transcend the shallow and raise our level of awareness and expand our purpose into something of greater meaning and value. We can choose to spread the goodness, or we can choose to be stingy. We neither change into a bad person nor do we transform into a good person when we come into prosperity. Rather, we become more of the chosen version of our self, and we attract more of that reflection in return.

Chapter Four

Envision

Envision: A Guided Meditation

Certainly, I realize that you cannot close your eyes and read this, so read through the following meditation, and then practice this experiential exercise. Alternatively, have a trusted friend very slowly read this page to you as you relax with your eyes closed. As a third alternative, slowly and in your most monotone voice, read this into a recorder and play it back when you're least likely to be interrupted, preferably as you're falling asleep. As you relax, your state of consciousness slows from the active 'busy-ness' level (which is Beta), to a slower (Alpha) state of consciousness. At the Alpha level, your subconscious mind is up to 200% more open to suggestions than it is while in the alert Beta State. It is for this reason that listening to a self-guided version of this meditation is most effective when listened to just as you begin to doze off for the night. At the level where Alpha meets Theta, you are most receptive to acceptance of the mental content.

Begin this meditation by closing your eyes…. Breathe in a deep breath through your nose. Hold it gently for a count of three, and then fully release the breath through your slightly open mouth. Repeat this focus on your breathing three times, consciously breathing in life-giving oxygen, holding it for a count of three, and then releasing any settled tenseness out with the exhaled breath…. One more time…breathe in through your nose…hold it for a count of three…exhale completely….

With your eyes still gently closed, imagine you are observing your ideal self standing in front of you. See you being the most perfect image of you. As you look at your ideal self, notice the details of how you appear both physically and emotionally.

Chasing Rabbits & I Am…
By Jan Deelstra

Answer the following:

- How is your posture?
- Are you standing in a relaxed or tense stance?
- What are you wearing?
- Are your clothes fitting for an ideal you?
- What does your face look like?
- Is your jaw tense or relaxed?
- Do you have scowl lines on your face between your eyes? If so, can you gently consciously relax your forehead?
- What are your eyes doing?
- In this image, are your fists open or closed?
- Are your palms sweaty or dry?
- What do you feel on your skin?
- Where are you?
- What environment are you in?
- What sounds do you hear?
- What do you smell?
- Who is with you?
- Are you alone?
- What does your automobile look like?
- Can you see it nearby in the driveway? What color is it? What condition is it in?
- Can you see your house? Where is your house? How big is it?

Open the door and walk inside of your ideal home….

- Look around; what do you see? What do you surround yourself with? What colors do you see?
- Is your home neat and tidy?
- Is it organized or disorganized?
- Who is inside your home?
- How does it feel to be home?

Continue to look around your desired home…

- How are you feeling both physically and emotionally?
- What is your jaw doing? Is it relaxed or tense?
- What are your hands doing? Are your fingers relaxed or are your fists clenched?
- How does your back feel?
- Are your shoulders proud or defeated?
- What is your heart telling you? Is your heart beating calmly or is it racing?
- Notice without judgment…just notice…. How are you breathing? Are you breathing?

As you look at this ideal of yourself, answer this question of what had to change from the old role you played to allow you to move into this new ideal image? Let that question settle in…you can journal it when your eyes are open. For now, just let it settle in…. What had to change in order for you to be this ideal you?
What shift took place?

Step into this ideal you. Merge your emotional and physical energy into this ideal. Feel yourself being your ideal self.

- Who are you?
- Who are you now being?
- Is this an authentic you?
- Are you aligned mentally, physically, spiritually, and aligned with your core values?
- Are your guts on board with the new image? Your solar plexus region will never let you down. It is your grand BS detector. Is your BS detector flashing any warnings or is it fully aligned with this new you?

Chasing Rabbits & I Am...
By Jan Deelstra

What does it mean to be this new self? Release any hold, move beyond the past remnants and be fully into the new ideal self.... Feel the full immersion into this new image of you. See you clearly wearing your new clothing; imagine you looking at your chosen automobile as it awaits you in your driveway... Imagine yourself living comfortably in your beautiful chosen dream home, living in your dream city, and loving your new inspiring career which is actually your divine calling....

Take in a deep breath, fully expanding your lungs and then fully emptying your lungs. Do this again. Breathe in deeply...and exhale fully....

When you are ready, walk to the door. Open the door and leave the home of your creation. Walk out into the sunlight, with the knowledge that you have changed. You have made the first shift in consciousness, to mindfully live the life of your desires.

Stand for a moment with the warmth of the day, illuminating you in front of your home...with your automobile parked nearby in the driveway.... See yourself in your chosen setting for one more moment. Feel yourself in your chosen setting....

When you are ready, and bringing with you that experience of being the ideal you as you have created that ideal, come back into this moment, and open your eyes. Allow a few minutes to be in the energy of this emotional state. Just be. How do you *feel*? Allow yourself to stay in the feeling until it subsides.

I recommend that you 'command' in the new version of you. Consciously create your new self and consciously move into this authentic identity through practice, clarity, and conscious creation of the new you. As you frequently invest the energy into this new vision of you, your subconscious feels the truth. You're raising your inner wealth and manifestation thermostat.

Be acutely aware of your feelings, physically, mentally, and emotionally. Set your tuner on the frequency you desire to *be*. Remember, fifteen to thirty seconds repeatedly held in this frequency brings swift shifts.

By practicing this format, you have consciously used the *Law of Attraction* to become the, "I AM" of your authentic calling and desired dreams.

There is limitless potential to transform into a higher vibration of the person you aspire to be, and through that raised frequency, to become wholly better in mind, body, and spirit. We are organic, malleable beings. Humans are as clay in the hands of the creator, and we are the creator. By successfully releasing internalized blocks from past experiences, we ease into the *I Am* that we are at a soul level. Mindfully holding that desired perfected image fertilizes the growth of the "I am." A daily practice of focusing on that raised self-image further cultivates an authentic and ultra-successful self. Consistently practicing this art of intentional creation will undoubtedly result in whole transformation.

Chase only one "rabbit" at a time until your desired result is achieved. Set your sights first on pursuing the one outcome which brings about the most authentic and rewarding *I Am* outcome of your *conscious* choice. Then direct your aim onto something even greater in the ladder of limitless potential.

~Ahimsa.

Chasing Rabbits & I Am...
By Jan Deelstra

http://www.JanDeelstra.com

About & From the Author Jan Deelstra

My own rabbit chasing began early. As a curious child, I was most often left on my own to seek adventure and pursue the deeper meanings of life. By the mid-eighties, I was a single mother, enrolled in college. I was also gainfully employed with the Department of Human Services, counseling a demographically diverse caseload of women. The multifaceted career exposed me to the deeper layers of the human condition, and ultimately transformed me, while simultaneously transforming the lives of my thousands of clients.

Fast forward to this moment decades later, my personal calling has evolved far beyond the walls of bureaucracy, into a richer, further diverse, global community of evolving women, each intent on discovering her true purpose and passionate calling. The layers are still rich and deep, and each woman I work with is still unique; every client is a precious gift in my life.

As the author of several personal development books, including the award winning, *Escaping the Chrysalis*, my mission to provide effective transformational tools to anyone within reach is now inspiring thousands more. The Internet provides the vehicle for delivery of empowerment services, and it simultaneously provides the means for your success, as you now consciously define it.

Chasing Rabbits is food for thought. It's offered to whet your appetite and encourage you to belly up to the smorgasbord of life, on *your* terms. Taste life as if you are at a luxury winery sampling the possibilities. And then, *decide*. Decide who you are and what you stand for, and what you will not stand for. Decide to own the whole of you, as you mindfully decide her to be. Self-awareness is empowering. Taking a close look at the 'self' allows for conscious enhancement of traits which empower, and allows for deciding which traits and habits to improve.

"Decide," translates to mean 'cut away'.

- Cut away the options until you get crystal clear on who you are now consciously choosing to be.
- Focus on honing and polishing the characteristics you appreciate in others, and clarify the values you will go to the mat to defend.
- Decide what to discard and what to enhance.
- Conduct all your actions and activities to reflect exactly who you are *being,* so that your passionate purpose and calling is in direct line with your actions and thoughts.
- Decide to surround yourself with only those who support and respect you.
- Decide to cut away the dead wood that keeps you stuck in the mire of the past.
- Decide to live your best life, and decide who you are being.
- It's your time now; *own it* fully, wholly.

http://www.JanDeelstra.com

To learn more about women's empowerment visit:

Other Books by Jan Deelstra: (All books are available on Amazon)

Escaping the Chrysalis: Introduction to Gestalt Techniques for Self-Esteem Transformation

This is the self-help manual you wish your parents had been raised with! It's not too late to save yourself, but this book is flying off the shelf so order yours now!

Learn to create the life of your greatest desires by letting go of the internalized blocks that stop you. Glean vital clues from your dreams. Reach the pinnacle of your potential.

ISBN 978-0-9885334-2-4

Blessings in the Mire: A True Story of Miracles & Recollections

Memoir meets spiritual self-help in this candid account of the author's attempts to make sense out of life and death and the in-between.

Many readers report a "healing" effect. We only know that it leaves us wanting more. It also leaves us with a ghostly haunting as we too contemplate the "blessings in the mire" of our own experiences.

ISBN 0-7414-3850-X

Shadows Attached: Mad Woman Poetry

The title says it all. This is a collection of some of the more feminist works of the author. The poetry is raw, and often brutal.

Attention parents: *Shadows Attached* is definitely <u>not</u> "kid stuff."

ISBN 978-0-9885334-6-2

(...continued....)

Other Books by Jan Deelstra: (All books are available on Amazon)

The Flying Game

After all she's been through, the endearing Stella Harris is understandably on the brink of disaster. But just when you think it's over….

Stella always won the "flying game." This time, she was playing for her life, and only the wisdom of Oz could save her….

A fictional journey that will reinforce YOUR determination to fly free of the chains that bind!

ISBN 978-0-9885334-7-9

Infinite Pie

Regardless of the current cultural climate around the state of the economy, there is plenty of pie to go around. In truth, the only place that scarcity exists is in mindset.

Utilize gestalt techniques to remove inner blocks to success and wealth.

Included are tools and techniques to have you attracting abundance, and experiencing financial freedom.

ISBN 978-0-9885334-8-6

See more titles and find downloads to support you on your journey at:

http://www.JanDeelstra.com

Thank you 🐰 ...often.

www.ingramcontent.com/pod-product-compliance
Lightning Source LLC
Chambersburg PA
CBHW051242170526
45165CB00004B/1538